Welcome to Basketball's Greatest Stories

Lunar Press is a privately-run publishing company that cares greatly about its content's accuracy.

If you notice any inaccuracies or have anything that you would like to discuss in the book, then please email us at lunarpresspublishers@gmail.com.

Enjoy!

© Copyright 2023 - All rights reserved.
The content contained within this book may not be reproduced, duplicated or transmitted without direct written permission from the author or the publisher.

Under no circumstances will any blame or legal responsibility be held against the publisher, or author, for any damages, reparation, or monetary loss due to the information contained within this book, either directly or indirectly.

Legal Notice:
This book is copyright protected. It is only for personal use. You cannot amend, distribute, sell, use, quote or paraphrase any part, or the content within this book, without the consent of the author or publisher.

Disclaimer Notice:
Please note the information contained within this document is for educational and entertainment purposes only. All effort has been executed to present accurate, up to date, reliable, complete information. No warranties of any kind are declared or implied. Readers acknowledge that the author is not engaged in the rendering of legal, financial, medical or professional advice. The content within this book has been derived from various sources. Please consult a licensed professional before attempting any techniques outlined in this book.

By reading this document, the reader agrees that under no circumstances is the author responsible for any losses, direct or indirect, that are incurred as a result of the use of the information contained within this document, including, but not limited to, errors, omissions, or inaccuracies.

CONTENTS

Inspirational Stories	8
J-Mac Breaks the Internet	11
Texas Western Take on Racism	16
CP3 Produces a Miracle	21
Derek Fisher and His Daughter	26
The Day Jordan Could Not Be Stopped	32
Rags to Riches Stories	36
Terry Rozier	38
Serge Ibaka	41
Caleb Swanigan	45
Jimmy Butler	49
Greatest Comebacks	53
The Kings Beat the Bulls, 2009	55
The Mavericks Beat the Timberwolves, 2008	58
The Jazz Beat the Nuggets, 1996	62
The Lakers Beat the Mavericks, 2002	65

Greatest Buzzer-Beaters — 69

John Stockton, 1997 Western Conference Finals, Game 6 — 71

Kawhi Leonard, 2019 Eastern Conference Semifinal, Game 7 — 74

Jerry West, 1970 NBA Finals, Game 3 — 77

Ralph Sampson, 1986 Western Conference Finals, Game 5 — 81

Greatest Upsets — 84

The Trail Blazers Beat the 76ers, 1977 NBA Finals — 86

The Warriors Beat the Mavericks, 2007 Western Conference First Round — 89

The Warriors Beat the Bullets, 1975 NBA Finals — 92

The Nuggets Beat the SuperSonics, 1994 playoffs — 95

Did You Know... — 98

The Final Buzzer — 104

Glossary — 107

INTRODUCTION

Welcome to the magical world of basketball and the brilliant stories it always seems to create. Throughout its long history, the National Basketball Association (NBA) has produced magical moments and tales that will live on forever. Sport is an amazing thing. It helps bring communities together, gives people a chance to make a success of themselves, and starts bonds that live on forever.

There are many levels of sports, from a kid picking up a ball for the first time to semi-pro athletes who do it because they love it to those who make it to the very top. In this case, that's the NBA. The highest level. The game played on the sacred boards of the world-famous arenas across America.

With such a high level as the NBA, brilliant moments are bound to be created on a regular basis. But it's not just those single bits of stardust that we are here to cover—we will cover them, too, don't worry!—but also the many other fantastic aspects of basketball and the NBA.

In our Rags-to-Riches Stories section, you will hear about Serge Ibaka, who escaped a war-torn country to excel in the NBA. The Greatest Comebacks section will have a 35-point flip that seemed impossible right up until the very last second. And we will have buzzer-beaters and classic upsets when the Davids of the league beat the Goliaths!

We will open with our inspirational stories, those uplifting moments and tales that remind us the world can be a pretty great place. They will make you smile, and they might even make you cry, but always in a joyful way! When we hear about people going above and beyond to make others happy or stepping up to the plate when nobody gives them a chance, it always warms our hearts. These inspirational stories will do just that!

Basketball and the NBA are so much more than glamorous players and fancy uniforms. It's all about a city coming together as one to support their favorite franchise, even if that team has lost 38 and won only 2 all season! We follow them because we love them, and even when things are going badly, they can still give us a memorable moment somewhere along the line.

That's why you might hear about some players or moments in this book that you never knew about, and that's always a great thing. Of course, you will see the names of the most famous players in history too. A book about basketball can't be written without the likes of Michael Jordan and the Bulls team of the 1990s getting a mention, just like it couldn't be without the Lakers, the Mavericks, and the Jazz appearing throughout.

Some of the things you'll read about happened over 40 years ago or more, so they might be new to you.

You're only young, so you won't have heard about everything that's happened in the NBA! Even adults who live and breathe the sport learn something they didn't know all the time. That's why we love the game—it never stops giving.

The NBA started in 1946, but there were many forms of basketball before then. Even when it began, there were rival leagues. Nowadays, the NBA is where it's at, and its popularity has caused the sport to spread far and wide. There are major leagues all across Europe, Africa, South America, Asia, and Oceania. It is a global sport.

So, even when we look back at all of the memorable moments in the NBA, we can't forget that other brilliant memories are constantly being made around the world! That's how special basketball is to those who play and watch it.

Our first section is Inspirational Stories. It's an excellent way for you to settle into what we're doing here, and we hope it will bring you some joy. The first buzzer is about to go, so make sure you're ready to play!

INSPIRATIONAL STORIES

Much like human beings, inspirational stories come in all shapes and sizes, yet they are all as important as each other. Inspirational stories can make us believe that anything is possible, while at other times, they just make us feel good about life. But something they all do is show us that life is pretty great and that we need to concentrate on the good stuff a little more.

A quick example is the story of Allan Guei, the teenager who won $40,000 in a free-throw competition and then shared it among the other contestants. Yep, you read that correctly. He gave the winnings away!

Allan was a top player for his high school—Compton High School, to be exact—who found himself in a free-throw competition that had been set up by a man named Court Crandall. And yes, you read that right. The man's first name was actually Court, and he was making a documentary about basketball!

Court Crandall has been a writer on many movies and TV shows. He was one of the creators of the blockbuster comedy Old School starring Will Ferrell, which won several awards. Warning, though. Unless you're 15 or over, you won't be able to watch it!

In 2011, Court Crandall decided to film a documentary about the importance of basketball in inner-city neighborhoods. He decided to open it with a free-throw competition with a $40,000 prize for the winner, and one of the names suggested to him was young Allan Guei. Allan agreed to take part, but some of the other participants weren't happy about it.

Allan was a high school basketball star, after all, and the rest of the kids only played for fun. They thought Allan's experience would give him an unfair advantage. In a way, they were right, as Allan won the whole thing!

In a brilliant twist, Allan would soon make one of the most generous gestures imaginable. And it was all captured on film.

You see, Allan had just been accepted into his dream college, Cal State Northridge, around the same time as the competition began. Still, he would have been well within his rights to keep the prize money for himself. College life isn't cheap, even on a basketball scholarship!

As Allan sank the winning basket, the other seven finalists grumbled among themselves that it was unfair. Amazingly, as Allan was handed his giant check for $40,000, he turned around and said he was going to share it with the other finalists!

As Allan put it, he had been blessed with his scholarship, so he didn't need the money. But he knew the other seven finalists also wanted to pursue their dreams. And that was it—he just wanted to help.

You don't get much more inspirational than that.

Allan's story can be seen in the movie Free Throw, along with the lives of the other seven young boys and girls who participated. The documentary is positive and sweet, much like Allan Guei himself!

Generosity is always inspirational, but inspiration can come in many forms, as you are about to see!

J-MAC BREAKS THE INTERNET

We will open our list with one of the most inspirational stories in any sport, not just basketball. It is a tale of bravery, passion, and of overcoming obstacles. It is a story that belongs on a movie screen, and as you'll soon see, that is what's going to happen in the near future!

Jason McElwain was born in Rochester, New York, on October 20, 1988. He was diagnosed with autism at the age of two and struggled to make friends and even be around other people in his early years. Like a lot of autistic children, he found socializing tough. When his older brother Josh introduced him to basketball, that all changed.

Jason McElwain, the boy who would become known the world over by his high school nickname J-Mac, adored basketball. Even though he had to attend special education classes in his early childhood, he never let it hold him back. He shot hoops after school with Josh and his friends, but it was hard for Jason to push through his social anxieties every time. His autism made it extremely difficult for him to handle the noise and constant interaction of a raucous game of basketball.

Still, Jason was always around the sport. He followed his brother's high school team, Greece Athena High

School, and he trained and hung out with the team in later years. It was around this time that he earned his nickname, J-Mac. It was a play on G-Mac, which had been the nickname of former Athena star player Gerry McNamara.

As Jason's confidence grew in his teen years, he became more and more involved with the Greece Athena High School team. He was around his teammates all the time, and the rest of the players loved his enthusiasm and passion. Also, they were fully aware of how good a player Jason was when he really let go on the court. Unfortunately, this wasn't easy for J-Mac due to his autism.

And that's how it went for Jason for a while. He loved basketball, loved the team, and loved the friends he made. When the team's coach, Jim Johnson, decided to make Jason manager, he was delighted. It was another remarkable achievement for a kid who once struggled to even make eye contact with other kids.

But J-Mac's special moment was still to come. That came on February 15, 2006.

In the lead-up to Athena's final game of the season, Coach Johnson had decided that he would put Jason on the bench. His plan was to bring J-Mac on for the last few minutes if the team had a healthy lead. That way, the boy who adored basketball and the Athena team would end the season with some minutes on the court and his own jersey to remember it by.

It was a decision that would soon become world news!

Spencerport was the opposition that day. A young Athena student named Marcus Luciano had been given the responsibility of recording the game from the bleachers since the regular guy was absent. It was another incident that day that just felt like it was fate. If the kid who usually recorded the games had shown up, then maybe the footage that went around the world in the days that followed might never have existed! But we'll get to that in a bit.

In one of the many other strokes of fate that day, Athena did manage to build up that healthy lead the coach had hoped for. Coach Johnson still waited until there were only four minutes and 19 seconds left before he made the call to bring J-Mac in, but as it turned out, that was more than enough time for him to light the place up!

As Jason stretched out and got ready to come into the game, the atmosphere was electric as the crowd's excitement spread through the stands. Jason was a popular kid who was adored for his kind heart and love of basketball. Still, when he finally joined the game, even his closest friends couldn't have predicted what would happen next.

Jason's first two attempts—a three-pointer and a failed layup—didn't quite work. He didn't give up, though. People with Jason's passion and mental strength don't know how to give up.

His next attempts became the stuff of legend, and he hit one of those unexplainable purple patches* that people in sports find once in a lifetime. Everything he touched turned to gold.

Amazingly, Jason sank six three-pointers and a two-point jump shot in his next seven attempts. It was magical, and with each score, the crowd went crazier. Marcus Luciano, the boy asked to record the game, was under strict instructions to only film the game's formations. Thankfully, he broke the rules, and after the crowd erupted for Jason's first three-pointer, Marcus began filming the crowd's reaction, then J-Mac, back to the crowd, then J-Mac again.

Even Coach Johnson, the man who asked him to record the formations, later admitted he was glad Marcus liked to break the rules!

When the buzzer went off at the end, the crowd rushed the court, lifting Jason onto their shoulders like he was the star of the movie Rudy. It was all caught on camera, and the footage would soon be shown on news channels around the globe. In fact, it was being beamed all over America by the time J-Mac sat down for breakfast the following morning.

The final score became secondary (Athena 79, Spencerport 43). The story was now about the unfair images we sometimes form of people without ever really knowing them. It was about the strength of the human spirit and how we can all come together as one when the time calls for it. But mostly, it was about J-Mac.

The boy who dreamed of playing basketball for his high school team but feared his autism would never allow it not only lived his dream but crushed it. He produced a magical moment that was talked about by NBA legends, actors, news anchors, and even the president of the United States. J-Mac caught the imagination of the world and let everyone who heard his story and watched the footage know that anything is possible if we believe.

Since that special day, J-Mac has become a celebrity. He has written an inspirational book and appeared on an endless number of chat shows and news channels. He gives speeches to massive crowds and helps those who listen believe that they can be whatever they want to be if they really go for it.

More recently, over 25 major movie companies, including Walt Disney, have fought over the rights to make a movie about Jason's life. I think we can all agree that is something we would love to see!

TEXAS WESTERN
TAKE ON RACISM

Now we have a completely different type of story, but one that is just as inspirational. It was also made into the movie Glory Road, and it is something that is sure to move you!

The year 1966 might seem like a long time ago to some, but in truth, it's barely a blip on the world's clock. Most of your grandparents would have been playing with their Stretch Armstrong toys and waiting for that other Armstrong, Neil, to walk on the moon around that time. So really, it's not that far back at all.

So how is it that in 1966, no college basketball team had ever consisted of only African American players in the starting five? At a time when America was building rockets that could fly to the moon, people still felt the need to separate Blacks from Whites. We can all be grateful that things have changed dramatically since then.

The Texas Western Miners played out of Texas Western College (soon to be called the University of Texas) and were run by Hall of Fame coach Don Haskins. The man who was nicknamed The Bear coached Texas Western for a staggering 38 years, from 1961 to 1999!

More importantly than that, he treated people as equals at a time when not many people did.

Like all stories involving racism, this one might be hard to hear, but it is important in life to know the mistakes of the past. If we ignore them, we will never learn to improve, and that would be tragic.

This moment in American history played out in the middle of the Civil Rights Movement, making the tensions felt around it so much more intense. For some, that 1966 Texas Miners team was fighting for the hopes of a whole race of people who dreamed of equal rights for all. The players faced a lot of hatred as well as plenty of love, but they were determined never to let the bad stuff drag them down.

There were White players on the team, but Coach Haskins refused to start them just to keep the racist section of the crowd happy. He picked his best starting five, who just so happened to be African American. That's the way he judged who should play for his team, and that's all anyone can ever ask for in this life—an equal opportunity.

That Texas Miners team was exceptional on the court, too, and Coach Haskins knew it. He had assembled a bunch of skillful players who also had an unbreakable will to win. By the time they reached the national championship final, they had lost just one game along the way, and that was only by two points.

Apart from that blip, they demolished every other

team they faced, winning their games by a 15.2-point average. Despite the racism they faced everywhere they played, they stuck together. By the time they came up against the Kentucky Wildcats in the final, they were ready to prove to the whole nation that segregation* was an awful thing that had no place in society.

That final against Kentucky is now seen as a massive moment for African American rights in the United States. In a disgusting twist, they were facing a team that didn't allow Blacks to play. The Wildcats were an all-White team.

Of course, such discrimination wouldn't be allowed today. But it is still shocking to know that less than 80 years ago, this was seen as okay. The Texas Miners players must have felt the pressure on their shoulders. It had to have registered that they were playing for every African American kid who had been rejected by a college because of the color of their skin. But if it did cause them stress, they didn't show it.

The Kentucky Wildcats were a dangerous team. By the time of the final, they were the number one ranked college team in America. Texas Western was third. The game took place at Cole Field House in Maryland, and much like the teams, the 14,253 people in attendance were split.

The starting five for the Texas Miners were Orsten Artis, Bobby Joe Hill, Willie Worsley, Harry Flournoy, and the master of the powerhouse dunk,

David "Daddy D" Lattin. They were ready to beat the so-called number one ranked team in the land.

After a cagey start, the Miners took control, building up a 16–11 advantage in the first quarter. They held their lead, and it was 34–31 at halftime.

The Wildcats tried to rally early in the second half, but the Miners were too slick. They made 26 of their 27 attempted free throws, pinning the Wildcats back and never once letting them equal the score. In the end, the Miners ran out 72–65 winners and completed a massively important moment in race relations in America.

In truth, the final score was never going to be the most important thing about that game. What really mattered was the publicity it brought and the awareness that such terrible things as segregation were still happening in America. Unfortunately, the racism the team faced continued after the game.

They weren't invited on the famous Ed Sullivan Show, which had always happened for every other team that won the national championship. The team also wasn't paraded through the town with their trophy, another thing that had always been done for the victorious teams before that game.

Still, positive changes did follow. The following year, the then extremely racist Southern Conference had its first African American player (1967), and the Miners managed to change the warped view that an all-Black team wouldn't have the discipline to win a tournament. Yep, you read that correctly. Some people actually believed that sort of nonsense!

After the championship, most of the Miners' players were ignored by the NBA Draft. Despite this, their legend will live on forever. They were the team that took on racist stereotypes* and ripped them up for all to see. They refused to back down, and the young men who stepped out onto that court in Maryland and demolished the Wildcats will be an inspiration for eternity.

CP3 PRODUCES A
MIRACLE

Chris Paul is known as a superstar in the NBA. He has amazed fans for years with his outstanding skills and his 12 NBA All-Star appearances. He was Rookie of the Year in 2006 and is a five-time Assist Leader and six-time Steal Leader in the NBA. Add a gold medal at the Olympics into the mix, and you have one heck of a basketball player. But these achievements shrink next to what he managed in his high school days.

Chris was born on May 6, 1985, in Winston-Salem, North Carolina. The boy that would become a world-class point guard for franchises such as the New Orleans Hornets, the Houston Rockets, the LA Clippers, and his current team, the Phoenix Suns, grew up in a loving family. His passion for basketball grew from the moment he first played the game, and his biggest fan was his grandfather, Nathaniel Jones.

Chris's grandfather was a hardworking man who taught Chris the fundamentals* of life. Nathaniel was also the first African American in North Carolina to own a gas station, something that made the whole family very proud. His work ethic* and determination rubbed off on young Chris, and it was something that drove him to become the man he is today.

When Chris was a kid, he was given the nickname CP3 because he had the same initials as his father and older brother. He was the third C.P. in the family, so he became CP3!

As a child and throughout his teens, Chris adored basketball. He described his grandfather as his best friend at the time, and Nathaniel used to close the garage early every time Chris had a basketball game. Nathaniel was one proud grandpa!

Chris attended West Forsyth High School and was soon being spoken of as a future NBA player. His dream was to go to Wake Forest University and make his grandfather proud, and days before his senior year, that dream came true.

Then, tragedy struck.

Five days after being accepted into Wake Forest, Nathaniel was killed outside his gas station. It was a senseless murder, and it devastated young Chris. His senior season was about to begin, and he would have to face it without his biggest supporter. Everyone around Chris told him to take some time off to deal with his loss, as he needed time to deal with Nathaniel's passing. Chris thought about it but decided that the best way to grieve—and honor his grandfather—was to play in the opening game.

On the eve of the game, Chris sat down with his beloved auntie and told her what he planned to do. She agreed that honoring Nathaniel in such a way would be a beautiful thing to do. She also would understand if it felt like too much for Chris to handle. He was just a teenager, after all.

But Chris insisted that he wanted to play for Nathaniel, and what happened afterward was like some sort of miracle.

After talking it out with his auntie, Chris suggested that scoring 61 points—one for every year of Nathaniel's life—might be the best way to honor him. His auntie agreed, but she feared he might be aiming too high. Chris's highest points tally in a single game before then had been 34. Now he wanted to score 61!

Fearing he might not make such a massive points tally, Chris didn't tell anyone else apart from his auntie what he was trying to achieve. The pressure was already so high without everyone knowing. He need not have worried. Something magical was about to happen, and Chris began racking up points for fun almost from the first buzzer.

He scored 24 points in the second quarter alone, and as each basket went in, the crowd started to whisper about what was at stake. Word had gotten out about his plan. Chris ignored the talk in the crowd and just concentrated on his game. He played so well that West Forsyth was out of sight by the end of the third quarter.

By the time the teams were getting ready for the fourth quarter, the crowd fully understood what Chris was doing. His parents were watching, too, and they could feel something truly special was happening. Chris stayed focused, but we can only imagine how he was feeling at the time. It must have been a powerful mix of sadness at his loss and tremendous pride in what he was doing for his grandfather. His best friend.

Chris kept scoring in the fourth quarter, but time was running out. With under two minutes left to go, he still needed six points to reach his goal. As the clock counted down, the crowd fell utterly silent. Even the other team looked on in awe as Chris tore around the court, desperately calling for the ball. He wanted—needed—to reach 61 points.

With a minute left, Chris made it 59 points, but he was still 2 points short. The seconds began to tick down as Chris received the ball just outside the paint. He drove for the hoop and was fouled, but the ball still managed to drop in. Chris had his 61 points!

He still had to take his free throw, though. If he got it, he would surpass the 61 he wanted to honor his grandfather, and that wouldn't work. He needed 61, exactly.

In a moment that would stay with everyone watching forever, Chris hurled the free throw out of bounds, then marched off the court to the ecstatic cheers of the crowd. He walked straight into his father's arms, who later said that Chris just let everything out at that moment. His love for his grandfather, his sadness that Nathaniel would never get to see him play for West Forest, and his pride at making 61 points—it all came flooding out.

Chris Paul, AKA CP3, did go on to play for Wake Forest University, and he smashed it. In his sophomore season, the team ranked number one in the United States for the first time in its history. By the time he left and went into the NBA Draft, he was a campus legend. Wake Forest retired his jersey in 2011.

A hugely successful NBA career followed, and as of writing this book, CP3 is still playing at the highest level. He is one of the highest-paid athletes in the world, a proud vegan, and a loving father. He is everything his grandfather knew he would be if he put the work in, which he did.

Chris Paul is an American success story and proof of what one person can do if they put their mind to it. But his most memorable and special moment came in front of a small crowd in his high school gym. It was the time he played for his grandfather and produced a miracle. We're sure Nathaniel was looking down on his grandson and smiling.

DEREK FISHER
& HIS DAUGHTER

Some things in life are more important than sports. These are the things we keep closest to our hearts—our parents, our siblings, and our kids. Our family. For any parent, the idea of their child being sick is enough to break their hearts. When that illness is something as devastating as cancer, then the pain is almost too much to bear.

When Derek Fisher found out that his daughter Tatum had been diagnosed with retinoblastoma, a rare form of cancer that affects the eye, he was devastated. Tatum was only 11 months old, and the thought of his precious baby having to fight something so serious must have torn the big man apart. But like her daddy, Tatum is a fighter. She came through her surgery as strong as ever.

But that's not the whole story. No, what happened around that time is what makes Tatum and Derek's tale so unique.

Derek Fisher has done it all in the world of basketball. He has won five NBA championships and numerous individual awards, including holding the record for the highest three-point average in the NBA. His glittering career has seen him star for the Los Angeles Lakers, the Golden State Warriors, Utah Jazz, the Dallas Mavericks, and the Oklahoma City

Thunder.

His famous shot with 0.4 seconds left on the clock for the Lakers against the Spurs was voted 18th on the Greatest Playoff Moments by the NBA, yet it was nothing compared to the one we're about to cover.

Derek Fisher was playing for the Utah Jazz in 2007. At the time, his team had just made it to the Western Conference Semifinal. What should have been a special moment for Derek was ripped apart when his daughter was diagnosed with retinoblastoma. From the second Derek got the tragic news, basketball didn't matter anymore.

With Tatum so young, the doctors insisted that the operation be done as soon as possible. There was a good chance that the cancer could spread and a real risk that her eye might need to be removed. It was a terrifying time for the Fishers. As the Jazz warmed up for the start of their semifinal series against Golden State, Derek was in a hospital in New York with his daughter.

On the day of Game 2 in the series—to be played in Salt Lake City—Derek was with his daughter as she went into surgery. He had secretly asked head coach Jerry Sloan to leave him on the active list for the game, even though he had no idea if he could make it.

Thankfully, Tatum came through her surgery with a clean bill of health. With time ticking away, Derek asked his wife if he should try to make the game.

Tatum was stable now, and Derek's family agreed—he should play.

Still, time was against him. Derek boarded a plane and headed straight for Salt Lake City. Even as he was in the air, the game had started. When he landed in Salt Lake, traffic was heavy, and Derek believed that making the game in time was now impossible. But he need not have worried.

When he stepped off the plane, he saw several police cars lined up. They were there to give him a police escort to the Vivint Arena!

With lights flashing and sirens blaring, Derek was sped through the city. His emotions must have been all over the place. The relief of his daughter pulling through and the leftover fear that something could have gone wrong must have been a lot to handle. Also, he had the added pressure of stepping in for his team while all this was going on. And in a playoff semifinal too!

By the time Derek arrived at the stadium, the game was already in the third quarter. During his police escort, Derek had been informed that starting point guard Deron Williams was in foul trouble, and the man being used as backup, Dee Brown, was injured.

The Jazz needed their best point guard more than ever.

As he walked into the stadium, Derek would have known how much the team needed him by the atmosphere in the crowd. He didn't even get a chance to sit down and had changed into his uniform in seconds. After that, it was straight down the tunnel.

The cheer as Derek came into view was like nothing the Vivint crowd had ever heard. Nobody there except for some of Derek's teammates and coaches knew the full story about Tatum. The people in attendance were aware that Derek had been in the hospital with one of his kids, but they didn't know the full details. Still, they knew that it had been a serious operation.

Seeing a man who had just been through all of that emerging from the tunnel to help his team didn't go unnoticed. The Jazz fans had always known they had a passionate and dedicated player in Derek Fisher, but this was something else.

Derek was brought into the game as soon as he was courtside. With barely any time left in the fourth quarter, he made an almost-impossible block on Baron Davis, which stopped him from making a game-winning shot. Derek's heroic block took the game to overtime.

He made another miraculous block in overtime, and this was followed by another magical moment. With the Jazz holding a three-point lead, Deron Williams found Derek in the open. The man who had been sitting by his daughter's bedside earlier that day sank a three-pointer, and the victory was sealed.

The crowd erupted, and Derek staggered into the embrace of his teammates. As he was being interviewed after the game, pure relief and joy could be seen all over his face. With tears falling down his cheeks, he told the world about his daughter's illness and how proud he was of her for pulling through.

It was a truly magical moment and one that made winning and losing seem unimportant. What mattered was Tatum's good health and nothing more. Still, shooting that basket in the last seconds of overtime was the perfect way for Derek to honor his daughter.

Derek Fisher only stayed with the Jazz for one year. After the scare he had with Tatum, he asked to be released from his contract at the end of the season. He wanted his family to be closer to the best hospitals available, and the Jazz agreed. The next season, he signed for the Lakers for a second time in his career.

These days Derek helps fund several cancer charities, and he raises money for families who might not be able to afford the type of top-notch medical care he was able to provide for his daughter. He has also coached, having been head coach for the New York Knicks and the Los Angeles Sparks.

Derek Fisher might have won five NBA Championships and be featured on the NBA's list of the Greatest Playoff Moments, but his most important personal moment came in 2007 when his daughter beat cancer.

Tatum gave him the one award that means more than any other for a parent. She made him a proud daddy.

THE DAY JORDAN
COULD NOT BE STOPPED

For many basketball fans, there will never be another player as good as Michael Jordan. He was a superstar like no other. His Chicago Bulls team of the 1990s blew everyone else away, and they made the NBA popular around the globe. They had other stars, too, such as Dennis Rodman and Scottie Pippen, but one player always seemed to be the one to make that killer shot. That man was Michael Jordan.

Coach Phil Jackson's Bulls had taken the NBA by storm when they won the franchise's first championships in 1991. They played a brand of basketball that was similar to the Lakers team of the 1980s—flamboyant* and attacking. Of all the Bulls' megastars, Michael Jordan stood head and shoulders above everyone else.

When the 1997 NBA Finals rolled around, the Bulls were looking for their fifth championship win in seven years. It was seen as the series that would cement that group of players as the best there ever was, and the Bulls wanted that more than anything.

Unfortunately, as the series progressed, Michael Jordan fell ill. He had the flu. But not just any flu. This illness had knocked him down. He was weak, nauseous, and faint. Every doctor the franchise asked him to speak to said he shouldn't play. He needed rest and lots of it.

In fact, Jordan was so struck down with illness that he didn't manage to sit up in bed until an hour and a half before tip-off time.

In the buildup to Game 5 against the Jazz (the scores were tied at 2–2), Jordan was as weak as a kitten. To add to his misery, he had gotten a bad case of food poisoning as well. He was in no fit state to lace his sneakers, never mind playing a game in an NBA Finals.

Yet Michael Jordan was irreplaceable. Phil Jackson knew it, and so did his teammates. When he said he was okay to play, nobody argued. If he could stand, he started.

If anyone in the crowd during that spectacular Game 5 hadn't known Jordan was sick, they sure did after the first five minutes. He was shaky and dazed and, at times, staggered when he tried to run. He shouldn't have been on that court.

But the second quarter came, and Jordan sprang into life. He scored 18 points in a powerful burst that made the weak-looking player from the previous quarter seem like a different person. The opposition players were clearly stunned, as they had settled into the game believing Jordan was finished for the day.

Unfortunately—or so it seemed!—Jordan had exhausted himself in the second quarter. He spent the third period much like he had the first: staggering around the court and missing easy jump shots. The flu and food poisoning appeared to be getting the better of him. It looked like even the great man was human, after all.

There was a moment in the third quarter when it actually looked like Jordan might collapse. He was dehydrated and shattered. It was clear that the Jazz would never have a better chance to take a 3-2 lead in the series.

And take the lead they did. They went into the fourth quarter with a handsome 77-69 lead. With Michael Jordan seemingly finished for the day, it looked like it was just a matter of the Jazz seeing the game out.

Jordan had other plans. He was about to play possibly the most miraculous quarter in the history of the NBA.

The game got flipped on its head as Jordan and his team took control. He scored seven points in a 10-0 point period for the Bulls, and the Jazz looked shell-shocked*. In minutes, the lead the Jazz had at the start of the fourth quarter was gone, and the Utah crowd at the Delta Center sensed that something special was happening.

The game went back and forth for a while, but the Bulls had gained a slight lead. With 25 seconds left on the clock, Jordan made a miraculous three-pointer to put the Bulls ahead 88-85. A Greg

34

Ostertag dunk brought the Jazz back within a point, but Luc Longley slammed in a dunk of his own at the buzzer to give the Bulls what seemed like an impossible victory, given Michael Jordan's illness.

As the buzzer went, Jordan collapsed into Scottie Pippen's arms, creating one of the true NBA magical moments. The image of Jordan slumped against his teammate is iconic, and it seems to show everything he had given for the team in one flash of a camera.

For a man that has won so many championships, scored an endless number of points, and is often called the GOAT* Michael Jordan didn't have many better games than that one. He has since admitted that it was the hardest thing he ever had to do on a basketball court, and that's saying something!

Jordan and his teammates have also said that he never should have played that night. He was far too sick. His coach agreed, but he also claimed that he could not have been the man to bench the greatest basketball player that ever lived.

Thankfully, Michael Jordan lived to fight another day. The Bulls went on to win the series, and the following year, they beat the Jazz again to make it six championships in eight years. They dominated the nineties, and a lot of that was down to the unbelievable talent of Michael Jordan.

RAGS TO RICHES STORIES

The second section of our book is dedicated to those rags-to-riches stories that show us the American Dream* at its best. They are the type of thing that makes us smile and believe that anything is possible. They inspire as much as the previous collection of wonderful tales, and they prove that anything is possible if you truly believe.

Rags-to-riches stories are often based on money-making ventures. Of course, that part comes into it a lot, but we need to concentrate on the achievement aspect of it. The men and women who make it in a sport when nobody gives them a chance are an inspiration. When they reach the highest level (in this case, the NBA), even though they grew up hungry, neglected, or in a broken home, they are the true rags-to-riches successes.

Then there are the people who came through hardships, poverty, war, and more to get to the very top. They set their mind on a dream and never stopped until they had it. Yes, they had setbacks and mistakes along the way, but these negative experiences make us who we are. They make us stronger.

Getting up when we fall down is what is truly brave. Saying to the world that you won't let anything stop you from finding your happiness and living your passion is what it's all about. There are many similar stories in the selection below, and they are happening all the time, even at this very second. In everyday life, people constantly battle the odds to come out on top when all seems lost.

For now, though, we will stick to the ones that relate to basketball!

TERRY ROZIER

Born into a rough neighborhood in Youngstown, Ohio, in 1994, Terry Rozier grew up knowing only struggle. His father, Terry Rozier Sr., was a criminal who had been in and out of jail his whole life. In fact, Terry Sr. was arrested and sent to prison for eight years around the time his son was born.

So, Terry basically grew up without a father. On top of that, he had to deal with teasing from the other kids, who made fun of him because his father was in prison. Like so many kids in the same situation, Terry found a release for his frustrations through sport. And boy, was he good!

Terry instantly became known around town as a super-talented kid. His skills were seen as his way out of poverty, and he was determined to make it for his family. His mother, Gina Tucker, worked a couple of jobs to make ends meet, and Terry spent a lot of time with his grandmother too. Alongside his brother and half-sister, they all made a home together.

Just as Terry's high school years were taking off, his father was released from prison. It must have been a strange time for Terry, as he would have had mixed emotions about what was happening. He loved his father, but there must have been a lot of anger in him too.

Things took a bad turn only a few months later when Terry Sr. was arrested, this time for robbery and kidnapping. He received 13 years in prison, and Terry had to deal with his heartbreak all over again.

Terry disappeared into basketball once more. In his senior year in high school, he averaged 22.6 points, 6.5 rebounds, 4.5 assists, and 4.7 steals. He also led his team to a 21-3 season, reaching the regional semifinals in the process.

But his father's negative influence had run deep. Terry struggled with his grades. He probably could have banked on his basketball talent taking him to college and beyond, but he has never been that sort of guy. He knew his education was the most important thing and that knowledge was key if he wanted to be the best he could be.

Taking positive action, he enrolled in Hargrave Military Academy for the rest of his schooling. Hargrave is a boarding school that is extremely strict on grades and learning. They also have an excellent basketball team!

Terry flourished in this stricter environment, and his grades improved dramatically. When he was done at Hargrave, he enrolled at the University of Louisville. He signed for the Boston Celtics out of college in 2015 and played with them until 2019. He had a brief spell at the Maine Red Claws before signing for the Hornets, where he still plays at the time of this book being written.

Terry Rozier is a brilliant player in the NBA and someone that millions of kids look up to. But his story is so much more than what he does on the court. He is a true rags-to-riches story and an inspiration in so many ways. He never let his circumstances take him down and actually used them to spur him on.

What a player. And what a person. Believe, like Terry Rozier, and you can achieve anything!

SERGE IBAKA

Now we have a man who came through a civil war as a child before going on to play in the NBA. Not just that, but he also became the first person from his homeland to ever play in the NBA. He grew up in poverty, on the run from rebel soldiers, and hungry. Yet, he kept standing tall. He never gave up. And he chased down his dream.

Serge Jonas Ibaka Ngobila was born on September 18, 1989, in Brazzaville, the People's Republic of the Congo (now just the Republic of the Congo). At a time when a civil war was ripping the country apart, the last thing expected of a young kid in the Congo was that they would one day play basketball in America. But that's precisely what Serge Ibaka did!

The third youngest kid in a massive family, Serge grew up in poverty with his 17 other siblings! They lived in a two-bedroom house with hardly enough money to feed two people, never mind a family of that size. Yet, the human spirit is the strongest part of us, and throughout history, people have come through terrible times to reach the top.

Despite everything that was going on, Serge still had a good introduction to basketball. His father played amateur ball for the men's Congolese national team, and his mother went one better, playing pro ball for the women's national team!

Unfortunately, Serge didn't get much time to practice with his mom. She passed away when he was young, but her influence on him stayed strong. And soon, more tragedy was about to strike the Ibaka family.

Not long after Serge's mother died, his father was imprisoned during the Second Congo War. It was a horrible time, and all Serge's father was guilty of was trying to sneak his family out of the country so they would avoid the violence of war. Serge and his siblings were left to fend for themselves.

Serge played junior basketball with his local team, Avenir du Rail. Not long after making his debut for the senior team, he left suddenly, joining cross-city rivals Inter Club. Both franchises play in the Congolese league, and his decision was met with anger. The Avenir du Rail fans knew they had lost a young man who would go on to do special things in basketball. They had never seen anything like him.

A powerful performance in the 2006 FIBA Africa Champions Cup brought Serge to the attention of some of Europe's biggest franchises. It wasn't long before he was on the move again.

His next stop was France, where he signed for L'Hospitalet in March 2007. He was just 17 and alone in a strange new city, but Serge was determined to make a career in basketball. His standout performances in France earned him a move to Spain, which has one of the best leagues in Europe.

While there, Serge's teammates marveled at how quickly he learned the language, something Serge as done many times in his life. They were also amazed at how good he was, and he became the team's star player after a couple of games.

Although he wasn't one of the first picks in the 2008 NBA Draft (he was 28th), the Seattle SuperSonics still believed they had unearthed a real gem. Six days after the draft, the SuperSonics rebranded and moved to Oklahoma City, becoming the Oklahoma City Thunder.

The franchise knew Serge was still a raw talent, and going straight into the NBA might stunt his growth as a player. He needed to get up to speed, and he was still young. They suggested he stay in Europe for three years to give him time to hone his skills. The NBA is a lot more challenging than the European leagues.

Serge signed a three-year contract with Ricoh Manresa of the ACB League in Spain in 2008, but he was flown over to the States a year later following some unbelievable performances for the Spaniards. Oklahoma paid his buy-out clause two years early, and Serge's influence in the NBA was almost instant.

He has played for several top franchises in the NBA since and won his first championship medal in 2019 with the Toronto Raptors. He also won a silver medal at the 2012 London Olympics, and he is still playing at the top level.

Outside of basketball, he is a talented chef who has his own popular channel on YouTube. He does a lot of charity work both in America and back in the Republic of the Congo. He is fluent in four languages and an all-round gentleman.

Serge Ibaka came through poverty, heartbreak, loss, and war to reach the NBA. He had a dream as a child that most people laughed at, yet he never gave up. When he was told that no Congolese person would ever make it in the NBA, he shrugged and said, "We'll see."

Serge never let the doubters win. His tale is one of the most inspiring rags-to-riches stories you are ever likely to hear!

CALEB SWANIGAN

This next person on the list might not be as well known as Terry Rozier or Serge Ibaka, but his story is just as inspiring. It ends tragically, but in life, we often need to concentrate on the uplifting parts, not the negative. Regardless of how things ended for Caleb, he came through so much struggle to make his star shine. It didn't light up the sky for long, but when it did, it was spectacular.

Caleb Sylvester Swanigan was born in Indianapolis, Indiana, on April 18, 1997. His home life was a constant struggle, and he lived on frozen dinners and candy. His father, Carl Sr., was a drug addict who struggled with obesity, and his mother was neglectful. Because of his bad diet and lack of exercise, Caleb's weight became a real problem in his childhood.

Throughout all of this, Caleb had to watch as he and his family suffered abuse at the hands of his father. Carl Sr. was arrested several times for assaulting his family before he died in 2014 due to his weight, drug addiction, and diabetes.

In the first ten years of Caleb's life, his mother moved the family around constantly, mostly in places around Utah and Indianapolis.

Caleb later recalled having lived in at least five different homeless shelters and attending 13 different schools before he reached his teen years. It was a very unstable childhood.

Also, Caleb had really started to put on weight by then. Like his father, he had an addictive personality. If he tried something he knew wasn't good for him, it didn't matter—he had to have more. Being fed nothing but frozen meals and fast food as a kid didn't help matters.

By the time Caleb had reached the eighth grade, he weighed 320 pounds.

Around this time, his mother finally settled the family in Houston, Texas. Fearing that he would die from his obesity if he didn't get help, Caleb's brother sought help from his old AAU basketball coach, Roosevelt Barnes. Roosevelt agreed to step in, but only if he was allowed to adopt Caleb. He knew Caleb needed a clean break from his home life if he was to get better.

Caleb moved in with Roosevelt, who became his legal guardian. Roosevelt started Caleb on a strict diet and exercise plan, and Caleb took to it with enthusiasm. He loved the intensity of working hard and the results it brought to his health and fitness. He felt better about himself.

When Caleb finished high school, he had lost over a hundred pounds, and his basketball skills had improved massively. He'd always been decent, but his weight had slowed him down. Now, he was a powerful and dynamic forward who was being watched by a lot of the top scouts.

After considering many different colleges, Caleb settled on Purdue University. He played some of his best basketball at Purdue, and the constant mix of classes, practice, and games kept his body in shape and his mind occupied. In other words, it kept him away from the bad things, such as fast food and drugs.

As we mentioned, Caleb's father had passed down his addictive personality. So, as long as Caleb stayed away from those things, he'd be okay. Unfortunately, it didn't work out that way in the end.

During his college years, Caleb won gold medals at the FIBA U17 and U19 World Championships in 2014 and 2015, respectively*. Unfortunately, some of the best times in his life came around the time he buried his father. It seemed like things were never going to be easy for Caleb Swanigan.

Caleb was a McDonald's All-American in 2015, and he finished college and entered the NBA draft in 2017. When the Portland Timberwolves drafted him, he claimed the moment was beyond his wildest dreams. The kid who weighed 320 pounds in the eighth grade had just signed for a top NBA franchise!

Sadly, this is where things started to go wrong for

Caleb. Injuries and temptation got the better of him, and he struggled to control his addictions. He bounced around a few different franchises over the next few years before a serious injury sidelined him for a long time.

While out injured, his eating habits deteriorated, and his weight shot up. When a picture showing his change in appearance went viral, online trolls picked Caleb apart. The abuse he suffered created a lot of media attention, which led to stricter punishments for people who bully online. But it was too little too late for Caleb. His spirit had been broken.

Caleb's NBA career ended before it really began, and he passed away due to his bad health in 2022. He was only 25.

His star might have burned out too soon, but Caleb Swanigan's story can light up the darkness for anyone. The pain he suffered as a kid should never happen to anyone, yet he found a way to get through it. Not only that, but he managed to go from an overweight teen to one of the hottest prospects in the 2017 NBA Draft!

He is a role model for anyone who thinks they can't improve their situation.

JIMMY BUTLER

From his father leaving him to his mother kicking him out for no reason when he was just 13, Jimmy Butler's childhood was one of pain and suffering. It would have been easy for him to give up—to think that he was just an unwanted kid—but inspirational people are made of sterner stuff than that. Jimmy always kept a positive mindset, and he made sure his dreams came true.

Jimmy Butler was born in Houston, Texas, on September 14, 1989. Only weeks after his birth, Jimmy's father packed up and left the family, leaving his mother to raise him. He grew up in a poor neighborhood in a town called Tomball, and there were often nights when he went to bed hungry.

But Jimmy found an escape in sports, especially basketball. When he was on the court, he wasn't just some poor kid from a broken home. He was Jimmy Butler III, a talented young small forward who could sink baskets for fun. He was somebody.

Jimmy's early childhood was a struggle. His mother was neglectful, and she took her anger at Jimmy's father out on her son. The tension at home forced Jimmy out onto the local courts more and more. He seemed to spend all his time shooting hoops.

When he was 13, Jimmy's mother kicked him out. She gave no explanation and just told him she didn't like the look of him anymore. Unbelievably, Jimmy claims to hold no grudges against his parents, despite the terrible way they treated him. That takes real class, and Jimmy Butler has a whole lot of that!

After being thrown out of his home, Jimmy spent the next few months bouncing around his friends' houses and bunking on their couches when their parents allowed it. It would have made him feel ashamed, even though none of it was his fault. Often the shame we feel in certain situations is completely wrong. There is nothing wrong with falling on hard times.

Remember, it takes real strength to ask for help. Bottling things up and going it alone never works.

In the summer before his senior year, Jimmy met a fellow teenager by the name of Jordan Leslie. Jordan was a star football and basketball player at Tomball High School who went on to have a brief career in the NFL. Jimmy and Jordan immediately became best friends.

Not long after their first meeting, Jordan asked his mother, Michelle Lambert, if Jimmy could move in with them. To Jimmy's shock, she instantly agreed. According to Jimmy, she did it only for the nicest of reasons. She was just a loving person who wanted to help and didn't care about all of the talk about Jimmy being a potential star NBA player one day.

Michelle already had six kids living at home, so when Jimmy was added, it was a pretty full house!

Still, that's what Jimmy liked most about it. He was surrounded by lots of people who loved each other. It was everything he ever dreamed of, and all under one roof.

Despite a great high school career, Jimmy wasn't heavily recruited by the top colleges. With his options limited, he chose Tyler Junior College, Texas.

His numbers continued to skyrocket at Tyler, and he was averaging 18.1 points, 7.7 rebounds, and 2.1 assists per game. This time, when he finished up, everyone was looking to sign him.

In the end, the Chicago Bulls won the race to get him. Jimmy played in Chicago from 2011 until 2017, being named an NBA All-Star and Most Improved Player in 2015. The following year, he won a gold medal at the 2016 Olympics in Rio de Janeiro as he helped the USA team to victory.

Following his time at the Bulls, Jimmy changed franchises a couple of times—the 76ers and the Timberwolves for a year apiece—before signing for the Miami Heat in 2019. He helped the Heat to the Eastern Conference Final in 2022, which they narrowly lost to the Boston Celtics. Jimmy's series-leader performance for the Heat wasn't enough to get them through to the playoff finals.

Jimmy Butler continues to be a major player in the NBA. He is also a successful businessman with his own coffee and clothing brands. His personality on and off the court is wonderful, and millions of fans around the world adore him. For the boy who must have thought nobody loved him growing up, that is quite a change.

When we think of someone being inspirational, people like Jimmy Butler fit that role perfectly. He had an awful childhood, but he never stopped believing. Yet his true success isn't what he's achieved in the NBA. No, what makes Jimmy Butler an extraordinary person is his ability to forgive all of those who hurt him in the past. He never held a grudge.

Now, that takes real courage.

GREATEST COMEBACKS

Comebacks are an interesting part of sports. They come in many forms—the last-minute equalizing point, the long, drawn-out clawing back of a game, and many more—but they are always exciting. Watching two teams switch the lead can be wonderful and painful to watch, depending on which team you love!

Even in games where we are neutral, the sight of a comeback can spark some intense emotions. On the one hand, it's great to see a team make a comeback. On the other hand, it's hard to watch a team slowly throw it away! Then there are the times when the underdog takes a huge lead, only to feel the pressure and start to let the lead slip. That can be hard to watch too!

In this section, we will have some mammoth comebacks. Sometimes it's not the size of the lead that's eaten up but the way in which it's done. Of course, most of the time, it is just a huge points difference being overturned!

Basketball is especially giving with classic comebacks through the years. There have been many, with each one meaning something different to the people who watched it. Because of the frantic speed basketball is played, comebacks can be pretty common. Even with half a minute left on the clock, the losing team can feel like they have a chance to turn things around.

A player can suddenly get a hot hand and rattle off 10 points without reply, or a team can suddenly feel the pressure as the winning line approaches and crumble. There are a million ways a comeback can happen, and all of them are as entertaining as each other.

We've selected four classics for you, so you can decide which one is the best!

THE KINGS THE BULLS BEAT 2009

This might just be the most remarkable comeback in the history of the NBA. In front of a shocked Chicago crowd, the Sacramento Kings overcame a 35-point deficit to claim one of the best victories ever. It ended up being Tyreke Evans's day, but he must have thought his team was on for a heavy defeat at one point.

For the Bulls, it was seen as a disastrous collapse, not a spectacular comeback. But that's the beauty of sports. One result can mean two completely different things to two sets of fans!

In a game that will be remembered for a long time, the first quarter belonged to the Bulls. They dominated, shooting 71% while holding the Kings to a weak 39%. The Bulls also committed zero turnovers. The second quarter brought much of the same, and the Bulls finished the half with a massive 67–43 lead.

But things changed in the second half!

In truth, the Bulls continued to play well early in the third quarter. With only 8:50 left on the clock, they were leading 79–44. Two minutes later, it was 83–50. The Kings looked dead and buried. But Tyreke Evans had other plans. His last-gasp heroics blew the

Bulls away, and their defense couldn't handle him.

The Kings went on a 19–5 run, dragging the score back to something a little more respectable. Then, with 31.1 seconds left in the third quarter, Evans made his two free throws, bringing the score to 67–86. The Bulls hit back, but Evans made a two-point shot at the buzzer to leave the score at the end of the third quarter at 88–69 Bulls.

Nobody in the arena would have given the Kings a chance as the teams got ready for the fourth quarter. Despite their gallant effort in the third, they were just too far behind. But Tyreke Evans had just been warming up. Now, the rookie guard was ready to steal the show.

Ime Udoka was another hero for the Kings that day, his two 23-foot three-pointers in the space of 40 seconds a particular highlight. He scored 15 of the King's first 22 points at the start of the fourth quarter, cutting the score to 91–95.

There was only 2:28 left on the clock!

Then it was time for Evans once more, as he personally outscored the Bulls 9–3 to give the Kings the lead for the first time in the game. The Bulls tried to fight back, but the Kings had the better of them by now.

The Bulls called a timeout with 14 seconds left on the clock and the Kings 100–98 ahead. Derrick Rose then missed a driving layup, and Beno Udrih picked up the defensive rebound. He drove with the ball, only to draw a foul from Kirk Hinrich. Udrih made both free throws, giving the Kings a 102–98 lead with just 5.5 seconds on the clock.

The Bulls didn't have enough time to respond.

The buzzer went, and most of the Kings and Bulls players collapsed to the ground. They had just taken part in a historical game and were exhausted. The Chicago crowd booed their team off the court, but the Kings players were ecstatic with their comeback.

Tyreke Evans finished the game with 23 points, but it was his all-around play that stood out the most. He might have been a rookie at the time, but he played like a seasoned pro.

We will cover more comebacks in this section, and all of them are amazing for different reasons. The time the Kings went to Chicago and overcame a 35-point deficit has to be one of the most impressive!

THE MAVERICKS BEAT
THE TIMBERWOLVES 2008

This game saw another massive overhaul of points, and the man who drove the comeback forward was a man by the name of Jason Terry. His performance in the second half was terrific, and he left the Timberwolves' defense in shock. No one player can win a game on their own, of course, and Terry's teammates all stepped up when the time came.

In fact, that game at the American Airlines Center in Dallas saw the most incredible comeback in the franchise's history.

There was more to it than just a simple comeback. Dallas went into the game as heavy favorites, so when the Timberwolves started to build up a lead, the Dallas fans weren't happy about it.

The Mavericks' defense was terrible in the first half, and the Timberwolves took full advantage. Al Jefferson was on fire in the first half, and the Mavericks couldn't handle him. His scoring made the home team look silly in front of their fans, who had already started to turn on their players. It was messy, which suited Minnesota.

Despite how badly the Dallas defense played, their offense was doing okay. At the end of the first quarter, the Timberwolves only had a seven-point lead. That is the type of lead that can realistically be recovered, and Dallas would have still felt like they could win the game. By halftime, they weren't as confident!

In the second quarter, the Timberwolves basically outscored the Mavericks two-to-one. Every time the home team thought they had pulled some points back, Minnesota would steal the ball, take it coast-to-coast, and stretch their lead. Then hit them again. By the time the teams took their refreshments at halftime, the Timberwolves had a 22-point lead!

To make matters worse, Dallas coach Rick Carlisle was ejected near the end of the second quarter for his behavior on the sideline. It was clear to anyone watching that he was feeling the pressure. His team had turned up that day expecting an easy win. Minnesota was making sure that didn't happen.

It has to be remembered that in the buildup to the game, Minnesota had lost ten straight games against Dallas. A low-scoring lead for the Timberwolves would have been a surprise. This was something completely shocking.

Unlike a lot of huge comebacks, Dallas didn't instantly fight back in the second half. In fact, the Timberwolves outscored them 8–1 in the first minute and a half of the third quarter. But that was pretty much the last burst they had. The Dallas assistant coach, Dwane Casey, tightened his team's defense, and the comeback began.

It started with a powerful dunk from star player Dirk Nowitzki, who had just had his nose busted open early in the third quarter. That set the Mavericks off on a 22-2 point run that dragged the score back to 63-72. From then on, it felt like Minnesota knew what was coming. Their players looked exhausted.

Jason Terry took control, scoring 24 of his 27 game points in the second half. In what was a flip of the second quarter, Dallas nearly outscored Minnesota two-to-one in the second half. The fourth quarter was especially dominant, with Terry and Nowitzki running the show. Minnesota couldn't get near them, and every shot seemed to be nothing but net.

As the comeback gained momentum, so did the crowd. For the first time, they could sense the victory. When Nowitzki made it 93-91 with another devastating dunk, Dallas had the lead for the first time. There was just over five minutes left on the clock.

Amazingly, the Timberwolves somehow found a short burst of energy and rallied for a brief period, but it seemed like nothing more than a desperate attempt. Dallas had all the momentum, and Minnesota looked lost. Still, when Al Jefferson sank a three-pointer to level the game again at 98-98, it seemed like the Timberwolves might hang in and scrape a result.

Then Nowitzki made a quick tip shot only seconds later, and Minnesota crumbled.

Dallas pulled away, and they were soon seven points ahead. The game finished 107–100, and the crowd erupted. In truth, the celebrations felt more like a huge sigh of relief than pure joy.

An exhausted Jason Terry told reporters that his team had left everything on the court. Nowitzki had a bloody nose, their coach had been ejected, and they had just pulled off a 29-point comeback. It was the biggest in the franchise's history and the largest lead lost in the Timberwolves' history too.

Some comebacks are memorable because the winning team was the underdog. In this case, the favorites won out in the end, but only after they fell 29 points behind!

THE JAZZ BEAT
THE NUGGETS 1996

Here we have another one where the team that was expected to win did just that, but only after letting their weaker opponents take a massive lead.

In 1996, the Utah Jazz had some real stars on its roster. Karl Malone and John Stockton (you will hear about him again in the Buzzer-Beaters section!) were two of the best players in the league. That Jazz team was the Bulls' biggest challenger in the late nineties, and if it hadn't been for the unbelievable talent of Michael Jordan and company, they probably would have won a lot more championships.

Coming into the game at the Vivint Arena (it was called the Delta Center at the time), the Jazz had a 10–2 record. On the flip side, the Nuggets had struggled, only racking up five victories in their first 15 games. With Utah also having a home advantage, this was seen as an easy win.

It didn't start that way, though. The Nuggets couldn't miss in the first quarter. Everything went in. Bryant Stith, Antonio McDyess, and Dale Ellis were electric from the first buzzer. In the opening quarter, they scored a combined 33 points, with an 86% shooting average. The Utah defense was chasing shadows.

By the end of the first quarter, the Nuggets had a massive 37–19 lead, and the home fans were livid*.

The second quarter brought much of the same. The Nuggets continued to dominate, and the Jazz looked like lost schoolchildren. Denver outscored Utah 34–17 to go into the locker room with a 71–36 lead at halftime. Karl Malone and John Stockton had both played terribly, and the whole Utah team looked defeated already.

The Nuggets scored again at the start of the second quarter, giving them a massive 36-point lead. It was seen as an impossible score to overturn. No team had ever come back from such a deficit in the history of the NBA. The Utah crowd booed their team off, and coach Jerry Sloan looked furious.

He later admitted that his team had been embarrassing in the first half, claiming that he felt the fans were right to boo them off the court. He let the players know how he felt at halftime, probably using several words that we can't repeat here! Whatever he said worked. His team performed a miracle in the second half.

As for his opposing coach Dick Motta, his locker room talk at halftime must have been easy, as his team was so far ahead. He later admitted that his players became overconfident. He said that, in the second half, they looked like deer in headlights. The ferocity of the Utah comeback caught them by surprise, and before they could do anything to stop what was happening, it was too late.

Karl Malone came out for the second half a different man. He blitzed the Nuggets, scoring 15 points in the third quarter. His teammates added another 16, and Utah finished the quarter outscoring Denver 36–15. It was a good performance, but they were still a long way behind.

The fourth quarter saw much of the same, with Malone continuing to dominate. He finished the game with 31 points and 10 rebounds, while Stockton did what he was best at—grabbing steals and racking up assists. The Nuggets had no answer, and they just had to try to keep Utah's relentless scoring as low as possible and hope their first-half lead wasn't eaten up by the time the final buzzer went.

In the end, they couldn't do it. The Jazz went on another roll in the fourth quarter, outscoring the Nuggets 35–17. It meant Utah had won the game 107–103, and the biggest points overhaul on record in the NBA had been completed.

For Bryant Stith and Dale Ellis, it was a heartbreaking result. They had fought so hard for the Nuggets in the first half and ended the game with 31 and 25 points, respectively. Stith had equaled the great Karl Malone's points tally for the game, but only one of them was celebrating.

Sports can be cruel sometimes, but it is also so rewarding. Winning and losing are a part of life. But when victory comes in such dramatic fashion as it did that night at the Vivint Arena, it always tastes so much sweeter!

THE LAKERS BEAT
THE MAVERICKS 2002

Once again, we have the Mavericks involved in a famous comeback. Only this time, they experienced the bitterness of being the team that threw the lead away rather than clawing it back.

When they met the Lakers at the Crypto.com arena (it was called the Staples Center at the time) in December of 2002, LA was the most dominant franchise in the country. They boasted superstars such as Kobe Bryant, Derek Fisher, and Shaquille O'Neal. They were the glamor team, who had taken over from the Bulls as the dominant force.

So, when they played against the Mavericks in front of their home fans, most people there expected the Lakers to cruise to victory. The Lakers did win, but they made a real meal of it!

A large part of the mess they found themselves in came from a bit of arrogance. The Mavericks were no pushovers. They had only lost once so far that season, and they would have quietly fancied their chances. The Lakers had underrated their opponents.

The first quarter wasn't as one-sided as some of our previous stories, but the Mavericks still took control. Steve Nash and Dirk Nowitzki both hit 25-foot three-pointers without reply in the space of 20 seconds before Raef LaFrentz did the same less than a minute later. Shaq tried to keep the Lakers in the game, but the Mavericks were really clicking.

By the end of the first quarter, the Mavericks were 29–24 ahead, but it could have been a lot more. In the second quarter, they really stepped their game up.

Dirk Nowitzki took control of the second quarter, and the Mavericks pulled further ahead. The Lakers had no response, and their fans were getting edgy. Fans jeered many of the Lakers' failed attempts, and the players must have wondered just what was happening. As we've seen in our other comeback stories, overconfidence can be a killer in sports.

LA had been superb for years, winning three NBA championships in a row. Their dominance over the Mavericks throughout the 1990s and into the 2000s must have played a part in their casual first-half approach too. They seemed to have expected the win before the first quarter even began.

When the buzzer went for halftime, it was 64–36 Mavericks. The boos from the LA crowd were deafening.

The Mavericks sensed that they were on for the franchise's first win against the Lakers in over a decade. Unfortunately for them, they were wrong!

Now, this is where it gets interesting. We are used to

big comebacks starting in the third quarter. It makes sense because teams need time to make up the points difference of such large deficits. But this game was different. In fact, the Mavericks kept the pressure on all through the third quarter. Despite a pretty decent quarter from Shaq and Kobe, the Mavericks still led by 27 points at the buzzer!

The Lakers were booed off again. The crowd knew a 27-point overhaul in a single quarter was almost impossible, even with Kobe on the team. But Kobe Bryant was always a man who loved making headlines. He was a winner, and he showed it that night.

The Lakers outscored the Mavericks 44–15 in the fourth quarter, with 21 of Kobe's 27 points coming in the final 11 minutes. Oh, and Kobe had also pulled his groin in the third quarter, just as his team fell 30 points behind. He performed his fourth-quarter heroics while injured!

He might have been taken off before then if he hadn't stopped trainer Gary Vitti from telling coach Phil Jackson. Kobe later said that he had to lie and tell the trainer he was fine. He wanted to play the rest of the game and help his team.

With under a minute left on the clock, Brian Shaw's turnaround jump shot made it 103 each. The Lakers somehow shot 16 of 18 from the field in the last quarter, and most of them were made by Kobe. Dallas then missed a couple of chances before Bryant went up the other end and made a 16-foot two-point shot. It was 105–103 Lakers with only 8.4 seconds remaining.

The Mavericks called a 20-second timeout, but it was too little too late. Their last offensive play came to nothing. Michael Finley missed a last-second three-pointer, and the buzzer went on an all-time classic.

Dallas guard Nick Van Exel was in no mood to mince his words during his post-match interview. He told reporters that his team had flat-out choked. There was no other way for him to put it.

Of course, the Lakers players would have disagreed. To them, their monumental effort had turned the game around. Either way, the Lakers' 27-point fourth-quarter turnaround was only one short of the record.

Sometimes in sports, it's the little details that make the difference. Dallas had some outstanding players, including Hall of Famer Dirk Nowitzki, Steve Nash, and Michael Finley. But the Lakers had Kobe and Shaq.

Sometimes, that extra bit of stardust is the game-changer!

GREATEST BUZZER-BEATERS

A buzzer-beater is one of the things that separates basketball from almost all other sports. When the clock stops, and only a few seconds remain, it's impossible not to feel our bodies tensing in anticipation. To see a player start his ascent into a jump shot as the final second ticks by and to know that what happens with the ball will decide which team feels the ultimate joy and who will be completely devastated is a powerful thing.

Sometimes, it feels like they belong to basketball. Other sports have buzzers, but none really end with the tense, magical moments the NBA produces. There is something special about the way a basketball game can end that sets up buzzer-beaters all the time, and that's something we should be grateful for as fans.

When we think of a proper buzzer-beater, it's hard not to picture Kawhi Leonard's shot that bounced on the rim four times before dropping. That kind of impossibly tense moment, as the whole arena paused and sucked in its breath, can't be repeated in any other sport. It felt like time had stood still.

There have been many buzzer-beater moments in

NBA history, but we are only going to cover four. Some you might agree with, and others, maybe not so much. It all depends on what each particular moment means to you personally. It can also come down to how important the game was, which player made the shot, and the teams involved.

Were they rivals? Had the team made a great comeback? Did the buzzer go in the split second that the ball left the player's hands?

These are all essential aspects of making a magical buzzer moment. It's only fitting that we open with one simply called "The Shot." You can't get more to the point than that!

So, sit back, and enjoy reading about some of the greatest moments ever produced on an NBA court.

JOHN STOCKTON, 1997 WESTERN CONFERENCE FINALS, GAME 6

We briefly mentioned John Stockton in the Greatest Comebacks section. He was the man who played with Karl Malone on that incredible Utah Jazz team of the late nineties. That same Jazz team might have won several championships if it hadn't been for the Bulls!

Stockton's historical moment came in the 1997 Western Conference Finals. Getting to the playoffs was nothing new for John. In his 19 seasons with Utah, his team made the playoffs every year. That just goes to show how good that team really was, as such an achievement is almost impossible.

When the Jazz came up against the Houston Rockets in the 1997 Finals, they were out for revenge. Houston had beaten them at the same stage in 1994, and Utah was still looking to make a first-ever NBA Finals. They'd missed out when they lost to the Seattle SuperSonics the previous year too.

Stockton and Malone were a devastating partnership. They both came into the team around the same time, and both played with the Jazz for nearly two decades. Also, the two of them finished the same year: 2003. So, it's easy to understand why they were so in sync on the court!

And they were never better than that 1996–97

campaign, helping the Jazz to a record 64 wins in the regular season.

They came up against a great Houston Rockets team that had Charles Barkley and Hakeem Olajuwon, among others, on its roster. The series was a see-saw event for the first five games, with the Jazz taking the first two and the Rockets hitting back in Games 3 and 4. The Jazz then took Game 5 to set up a real classic in the sixth.

Stockton performed brilliantly in Game 6, scoring 25 points and dishing out 13 assists, but he saved his best for last—literally. His buzzer-beater was quite literally the last shot of the Finals.

And here is how it happened!

With tensions at boiling point, the Rockets missed a two-point shot, and Utah called a timeout. There were only 2.5 seconds left on the clock, and the game was tied at 100–100. It couldn't get any more dramatic, surely? Of course, it did. And it was something to behold!

Bryon Russell inbounded at half-court, passing the ball to Stockton. With less than a second remaining, he jumped over Rockets' star player Charles Barkley to sink a near-perfect three-pointer that sent the Utah players wild!

The Jazz had made it to the NBA Finals for the first time in the franchise's history, and they had done it in the most dramatic fashion imaginable. They lost to the Bulls in the finals and then again at the same stage the following year (the one that completed Chicago's three-peat), but John Stockton had still created an NBA moment that would last through the ages.

He achieved a lot in his career, but that shot will surely always be his favorite!

KAWHI LEONARD, 2019 EASTERN CONFERENCE SEMIFINAL, GAME 7

We couldn't have a list of buzzer-beaters without including Kawhi Leonard's unbelievable effort when he helped the Toronto Raptors beat the Philadelphia 76ers in 2019. Why? Because it was the first-ever Game 7 buzzer-beater. It was a moment that literally couldn't come any later in a series!

Kawhi Leonard is a two-time NBA champion, and he's still playing, so it could end up being even more. The man nicknamed Claw, due to his masterful handling of the ball, has always been known as an extremely calm and collected player. His buzzer-beater that night saw him unleash a scream of joy that seemed to shatter that particular view!

After a highly successful eight years with the San Antonio Spurs, an injury-ravaged 2018 caused the Spurs to think they might be better off unloading Leonard on another franchise. It proved to be a big mistake. Leonard still had a lot to offer, as we will see.

Despite Leonard's obvious talent, his move to Toronto was seen as a risk for the franchise. But in his first game of the season, he scored 24 points and had 12 rebounds in a 116–104 victory over the Cleveland Cavaliers. After that, he went on a run of scoring at least 20 points in 22 consecutive games. It was the best run of his career so far!

He continued his unbelievable form into the Eastern Conference Semifinals against the 76ers. In Game 1, he broke another personal record, scoring 45 points in a single game. He was on fire, and the Spurs must have been looking on and wondering just why they let him go.

The series went back and forth until it was tied at 3–3 going into Game 7. Leonard had been immense the whole season, but his special moment was yet to come.

With 4.2 seconds left on the clock, the game was tied at 90–90. Leonard already had 39 points on the board, but he wasn't finished. The crowd in the Scotiabank Arena in Toronto held its breath as Leonard collected the inbound pass. He dragged Ben Simmons across the court before making a stretching jump shot that looked close to impossible.

The ball bounced on the rim four times as everyone in the arena held their breath. Then it dropped, and everyone went crazy. Kawhi Leonard let out a roar that was so out of character but completely natural. He had just made a shot that would live on for eternity, and it had happened with the buzzer going off as the ball bounced around the rim.

It was like something out of Hollywood. It was the stuff of dreams. And it was all done by a player the Spurs thought was past his prime.

The Raptors went on to the NBA Finals, where they played the Golden State Warriors. Again, Leonard was immense, picking up the Finals MVP for the second time in his career. Toronto won the series 4–2 to collect the only NBA championship in the franchise's history. It was Leonard's second, having won it—and the Finals MVP award!—with the Spurs in 2014.

Kawhi Leonard is still playing in the NBA at the time of this book being written, starring for the LA Clippers. He has plenty of years left in him, so who knows what more will happen with his career. Still, it's hard to imagine he will ever experience another moment as dramatic as the buzzer-beater in Toronto that night.

How could he? It was the last second in Game 7!

JERRY WEST, 1970 NBA FINALS, GAME 3

So far, our buzzer-beaters have both been in conference games. Now, we have one in the actual NBA Finals. The holy grail. The place where heroes are made.

Unfortunately for Jerry West, his fantastic moment didn't lead to victory in the series. In fact, it didn't even lead to his team winning the game, but it was still one of the most extraordinary scenes on a basketball court. To make it even more special, the 1970 NBA Finals was the first to be shown in full nationally.

Jerry West was a one-franchise player. He stayed with the Los Angeles Lakers throughout his 14-year career, managing to win the NBA championship in 1972, two years after his buzzer-beater. In between his highly successful time with the Lakers, he also picked up a gold medal at the 1960 Summer Olympics in Rome.

Nicknamed Mr. Clutch because of his big game performances, Jerry West also showed up in the so-called smaller games, which is proven by the fact that he was an NBA All-Star in every season he played professionally. He was designed for moments like his 60-yard buzzer-beater against the New York Knicks.

Growing up, Jerry shied away from attention. He was soft-spoken and had a high-pitched voice that caused the other kids to tease him. It took making it in the NBA for him to come out of his shell a little. And boy, how he did that night in the Staples Center.

The Lakers had won many championships by 1970, but they had all come in the late forties and fifties. By the time they played the Knicks that season, it had been 16 years since their last title. As for the Knicks, they had never won it.

New York had a strong team, but they were gritty. Their style of play separated fans, with a lot of neutrals rooting for the more glamorous Lakers, who had players like all-time great Wilt Chamberlain on their roster. Unfortunately for Wilt, he had missed most of the season after busting his knee, so the Lakers getting to the Finals that year was actually a bit of a shock.

But Jerry West had stepped into Chamberlain's position effortlessly—averaging 31.2 points per game—and his performances had carried the Lakers through. Chamberlain was fit for the finals, which meant that West was pushed back into his normal position as a point guard.

It all meant that the Knicks and the Lakers were meeting in the Finals for the first time in NBA history. It was Beauty versus the Beast. David and Goliath. It was the type of matchup that had a little something for everybody!

Game 1 was played at Madison Square Garden, and the Knicks won it comfortably. Game 2 saw the Lakers return to the Garden and take it to the hosts, winning 105–103 to level the series, making Game 3 all the more exciting.

Much like the first two games of the series, Game 3 itself was a see-saw affair. Both teams traded blows throughout, and it could have gone either way. Wilt Chamberlain was clearly still injured, so he was only operating on a half tank, but he was still effective. It leveled things up a little, which made for a more exciting game.

With just three seconds left on the clock, Dave DeBusschere hit a jump shot to give the Knicks a 102–100 lead. It looked to all the world that the Knicks were going to take a 2–1 lead going into Game 4. Of course, as we know, Jerry West hadn't read the script. In fact, he was determined to write his own!

Chamberlain quickly inbounded to Jerry West, who carried the ball a few steps before launching a 60-foot shot that didn't even touch the rim! It was an unbelievable moment and one that would have given the Lakers victory years later. Unfortunately for them, the NBA didn't introduce the three-point rule until the 1979–80 season, so West's amazing shot only counted as two points.

The game went to overtime, and the Knicks won it. They then went on to shock the Lakers by winning the series, but Jerry West's buzzer-beater will live on for a long, long time.

Sometimes magical moments don't end with the reward they deserve. In this case, that was true more than ever!

RALPH SAMPSON, 1986 WESTERN CONFERENCE FINALS, GAME 5

In 1986, the Houston Rockets were known as a good but not a great franchise. They had yet to win a championship, and reaching the Conference playoffs was seen as a massive achievement. It wasn't until Ralph Sampson (7-foot 4-inches) and Hakeem "The Dream" Olajuwon (7-foot) were paired together in 1984 that Houston became a genuine force.

The two massive men in front court became known as the Twin Towers, but people questioned whether a team could work with such size in one position. They were soon proved very wrong, and the Sampson-Olajuwon partnership is still seen as one of the best of all time.

Ralph Sampson was a three-time college national player of the year when he was the first overall pick for the Rockets in the 1983 NBA Draft. He would end up spending four seasons there, in what is often seen as the franchise's best period. The Dream was the first overall pick in the 1984 draft, and the Rockets began to improve every year.

The 1985–86 season saw Houston win the Midwest Division for only the second time. They finished with a 51–31 record, with Sampson and Olajuwon bossing the front line.

They swept the Sacramento Kings in the playoffs but then faced much more formidable opponents in the semifinals. The Denver Nuggets were an outstanding team, so when the Rockets beat them 4–2 to reach the Western Conference Finals, people had to finally sit up and take notice.

But things were never going to get easier, and the Rockets knew that when they came up against the Los Angeles Lakers in the Conference Finals. Remember, this is the Lakers team that won five NBA Championships in the 1980s!

True to form, the Lakers won Game 1, a comfortable 119–107 victory at The Forum. It looked like normal service had been resumed.

But Houston roared back, winning the next three games (one at The Forum and the other two at The Summit) to make it 3–1 to the Rockets. They hadn't just scraped by the Lakers, either. The Rockets had won all three games by at least eight points.

What would end up being the final game in the series was played at The Forum, the arena that had become a hot spot* for celebrity stars and famous musicians. The Lakers were seen as unbeatable there, and even though the Rockets had already won Game 2 in LA, people still expected the Lakers to take control.

Throughout the series, Ralph Sampson and Hakeem Olajuwon battled it out with the Lakers' star duo of Magic Johnson and Kareem Abdul-Jabbar. In each game, all four of them played superbly, so when Olajuwon was ejected in the fourth quarter of Game 5 for fighting with Lakers' player Mitch Kupchak, LA became favorites to win.

Ralph Sampson had other plans.

With Game 5 tied at 112–112 and only one second left on the clock, Sampson received a half-court inbound mid-air, spinning and getting off a twisting jumper that bounced twice on the rim before finally dropping in. The Forum crowd was stunned, but the Rockets' players went crazy.

It was a pure NBA moment and one that sent the Rockets into their second NBA Finals. Unfortunately, they would have to wait for their first title. They came up against a Larry Bird-inspired Boston Celtics, who had five future Hall of Famers on their roster. The Celtics won the series 4–2, but Sampson's buzzer-beater was the moment of the season.

For some, it's the most incredible moment ever.

GREATEST UPSETS

Upsets are a strange thing in sports. They are brilliant because it's the underdog winning. It's the team or player nobody expected to succeed. We all love sporting upsets because they make us believe anything is possible.

Basketball has had its fair share of unbelievable upsets. Some of them were single games, while others were series victories, making the result even more astounding. For a less-favored team to win a series, they have to keep upsetting the odds in every game. It's not just a one-off chance that they stole at the buzzer.

Of course, those moments are spectacular, too, as we've seen in our previous section. But when a bottom seed defeats a top seed, everyone gets a little bit excited. Well, everyone except the players and fans of the team that lost!

We will concentrate on the playoffs and the teams that won even though they went into the series with a much weaker regular season record.

In NBA history, the eighth seed has beaten the number one seed only six times. That's how rare it can be. So, with that in mind, we have to understand just how amazing a big upset is in professional basketball. Not only is the favorite usually a much better team according to its stacked roster, but they also have momentum going into the series!

Take our second entry in this section, for instance. One team went into the playoffs with a 67–14 record, while the other one finished the regular season with a 42–40 record. Now, we all know what team should win that playoff game, right? Wrong! It produced a mind-boggling upset.

Buzzer-beaters, comebacks, and inspirational stories are why we watch basketball. Following our favorite team and watching their games is great, and when we witness one of these special moments, we feel a part of it. In a way we are because those moments, victories, and losses mean nothing without the fans. It's the crowd's reaction and the videos posted online of families celebrating in front of the TV that make sports so special.

We couldn't fit all of the fantastic comebacks the NBA has produced in this section, but here are four we think you'll really love. Enjoy!

THE TRAIL BLAZERS BEAT THE 76ERS, 1977 NBA FINALS

The Trail Blazers had only been founded in 1970, so the franchise was only seven years old when it won its first—and only—NBA Championship. Before that 1976-77 season, the team had struggled to attract crowds of over 10,000, but they saw some rise in support when they drafted Bill Walton in '74.

The 1977 Finals victory over the Philadelphia 76ers isn't the whole story of an upset. That began with the first throw of the 1976–77 season. You see, before that year, the Trail Blazers had never posted a winning season. So, the first time they did so was also the time they went on to win the lot. The whole season was one big upset!

But when they came up against the Sixers in the NBA Finals, everyone apart from the Portland players and staff believed the fairytale run was over. Philadelphia's roster was stacked, with star players such as Julius Erving, George McGinnis, and Darryl Dawkins. They were expected to sweep their lesser opponents.

As for Portland, most of their players weren't long out of college. Bill Walton was the team's leader, and he worked miracles that season. Even with Herm Gilliam and Maurice Lucas, the Trail Blazers should have wilted under the pressure. Of course, they did no such thing!

The pre-series predictions of a Philadelphia landslide victory looked spot on after the first two games. But both games had been played in Philly, and the Sixers had gotten cocky. When they arrived at the Memorial Coliseum in Portland for Game 3, they were blown away by the hosts.

Bill Walton was immense, blocking almost every shot the Sixers attempted. Portland took an early 17-point lead and never looked back. The game finished in a 130–98 victory for the Trail Blazers.

They then went on to blitz a shell-shocked Philadelphia in Games 4 and 5 (winning Game 5 in the Philadelphia Spectrum!), setting up an unthinkable chance of winning the Finals in Game 6. The game was played in Portland, which only added to the Trail Blazers' belief that they could do it.

And they did, in the most dramatic fashion.

By now, the term "Blazermania" had become popular. The 1976-77 season had seen to that. The franchise that had struggled to fill its arena now had fans queuing up outside without tickets. It was a massive switch, and the effects are still felt today. Portland has one of the most loyal fanbases in the NBA.

Game 6 was a classic, with both teams on the offense from the first buzzer. Philadelphia struggled with the frenetic pace and the electric atmosphere in the arena. By halftime, they were 15 points down. Erving fought back, dragging the Sixers into the final seconds of the fourth quarter with only two points left to tie the game.

With four seconds left, a different kind of buzzer moment played out. The score was Philadelphia 107–109 Portland, and the Sixers inbounded the ball with just five seconds left. McGinnis drove the ball, but his shot fell short just as the final buzzer went.

Portland had done it, and in dominating fashion too. They had won four games in a row to take the NBA Finals 4–2. In most post-match interviews, Bill Walton's Finals MVP performance was hailed by both Portland and Sixers players and coaches. He was unbelievable throughout, and he led his team to their one and only NBA Championship.

It is possibly the greatest season upset there ever was and one that will be hard to beat!

THE WARRIORS BEAT THE MAVERICKS, 2007 WESTERN CONFERENCE FIRST ROUND

Unlike our previous entry, where a team managed to upset the odds at different times throughout a season, this is a moment that just shouldn't be able to happen!

The season records between the two teams in the lead-up to the series couldn't have been more different. The Mavericks were the number one seed, boasting a massive 67–14 record. Golden State had barely scraped through with a 42–40. This is why the upset was so shocking.

It was the first time the struggling Warriors had qualified for the playoffs since 1994. Following the Mavericks' near-record-breaking season, they were expected to win their first-ever NBA Championship. It was seen as only a matter of time.

But it wasn't just the fact that the Warriors beat the Mavericks; it was the manner in which they did it. They smashed Dallas to pieces.

Baron Davis was brilliant throughout the series, and in Game 1, he blew Dallas away. He only just missed out on a triple-double as he helped Golden State to a 97–85 victory at the American Airlines Center in Dallas. Beating the number one seeds on their home court sent a message, but it was one Dallas refused to accept.

The Mavericks put up a fight in Game 2, which eased the home crowd's nerves a little. But that victory seemed to make Dallas complacent*. They showed up in Oakland overconfident, and the Warriors made them pay.

Two comfortable wins at the Oracle Arena gave Oakland a 3–1 lead in the series, and suddenly Dallas looked scared. They knew they needed to win the next three, whereas their opponents required only a single victory to clinch one of the biggest upsets in NBA history.

Again, the Mavericks put up a bit of a fight when needed, winning Game 5 in Dallas. But it was too little too late. Even with the series at 2–3 now, Dallas knew they had to travel to Oakland for Game 6, and they had been picked apart there in Games 3 and 4. The Golden State players knew that, too, and they took full advantage.

Game 6 was a landslide, with Baron Davis breaking up every play Dallas attempted and the rest of the Oakland players performing at their best. Dallas had no answers, and the Warriors cruised to a 111–86 victory in front of 20,677 fans to win the series. It was not just an upset; it was a demolition job.

Unfortunately, Golden State's purple patch didn't last. Utah beat them in the next round, but that only helped to prove even more so what an upset it had been in the previous series. The top seed in the Western Conference had been smashed by the bottom seed. That doesn't happen often, and rarely in such a dominating way!

Everyone loves an underdog story. The Golden State Warriors team of 2007 gave us a classic.

THE WARRIORS BEAT THE BULLETS, 1975 NBA FINALS

This was the Golden State Warriors' third NBA Finals in the franchise's history and the first since their move to Oakland. The Washington Bullets were playing in their second-ever Finals, which became a habit of theirs in the seventies. All in all, the Bullets appeared in four Finals that decade, making them one of the most feared franchises at the time.

Despite the Warrior's good performance in the Western Conference, they were still second favorites for the Finals. The Bullets had a home advantage, and most people expected them to brush Golden State aside. The opposite happened, and the Warriors completed the first-ever Finals sweep for a team without home advantage.

In fact, it is such a bizarre event that it's only happened once since.

Golden State had only just scraped through in their playoff series against the Bulls, with rookie Phil Smith saving them in Game 7. Also, the Bullets had beaten them 3–1 in the regular season and then taken out the mighty Celtics in the playoffs, so the momentum was all with Washington.

To make matters worse for Golden State, they were forced to play their home games away from the

Oakland Coliseum, a place where the crowd was intimidating to the away team. The Coliseum was being used by the Ice Follies, a traveling ice show that was kind of like the Ice Capades. So, the Warriors were forced to play at nearby Cow Palace. Not the scariest of names for an arena!

Phil Smith was the hero again in Game 1 of the Finals. After Washington had taken a 14-point lead in front of their home fans, the Warriors roared back, with Smith scoring 20 points in 31 minutes after coming off the bench. The Warriors won the game 101–95, shocking the Bullets.

Game 2 at the Cow Palace was a tighter affair. A back-and-forth game saw the Bullets take a big early lead again, this time by 13 points. But once more, they threw it away. Rick Barry was the star this time for Golden State, scoring 36 points. The Warriors took a 92–91 lead with just six seconds left. When the Bullets missed two shots before the buzzer, Golden State had the victory. It was 2–0.

By Game 3, the pressure was really on Washington. They had been expected to sweep Golden State, but now they were the ones getting beaten. Rick Barry stepped up once more, this time bettering his Game 2 total by 2 points to finish with 38. The Golden State bench performed miracles, and Jamaal Wilkes shackled the Bullets' power forward, Elvin Hayes, all throughout the game. Wilkes had dominated Hayes in the series, limiting him to 29 points over the first three games.

The series returned to Washington for Game 4, with the Bullets 0–3 behind. Nobody had expected such a score, and Golden State was in no mood to ease up on the gas. Yet again, the Bullets took an early 14-point lead, but they seemed unable to learn their lesson from the previous games. Okay, so they held the lead for longer this time but still blew it with only seconds left to lift Golden State to a 96–95 victory.

It was the clean sweep everyone expected, but the other way around!

Rick Barry was named Finals MVP for his brilliant performances, and Golden State would go on to retire his number years later. The Warriors had won their third championship, something the franchise wouldn't do again for 40 years!

That 1975 NBA Finals is still seen as one of the biggest upsets ever. Not so much because the Golden State Warriors won it, but in the way they won it. A 4–3 victory in the series would have been surprising. Their 4–0 sweep was unheard of up until that point!

THE NUGGETS BEAT THE SUPERSONICS, 1994 PLAYOFFS

This one resembles the time the Golden State Warriors beat the Dallas Mavericks in 2007, in that the winning team finished the regular season with a poor 42–40 record. The Denver Nuggets barely made the playoffs, and nobody gave them a prayer. Compared to their opponents—the SuperSonics had won the Western Conference with a staggering 63–19 record—they were expected to get swept away.

In the end, the underdogs prevailed. It would be the first time in NBA history that the eighth seed beat the first seed in the playoffs.

This classic series could have made several of our sections. It did involve a massive upset, but it also had a win in the last few seconds and an astonishing comeback. It had a little bit of everything!

The Seattle SuperSonics had built that 1993–94 team around a rock-solid defense, with Hall of Famer point guard Gary Payton an unbreakable rock. They also had power forward Shawn Kemp, who was enjoying one of the best seasons of his career. The SuperSonics were many people's pick for the championship.

The Denver Nuggets couldn't have had a more opposite season if they tried. It started to go wrong before it really began when they traded Marcus

Liberty (what a brilliant last name!) and Mark Macon to the Detroit Pistons, exchanging them for All-Star guard Alvin Robertson. It looked like a shrewd trade, but Robertson injured his back before his feet even touched the court, and he never played a single minute for the Nuggets.

Given all of this, a Nuggets win was seen as an impossibility. Seattle had the home advantage, and they did what everybody expected in the first two games and won them comfortably. In a best-of-five series, having the first two games at home makes a huge difference. Everything seemed to be stacked against Denver.

Game 3 was the first to be played in Denver, and the 17,171 people packed into the McNichols Sports Arena were served up a treat. Reggie Williams's 31 points for the Nuggets saw them stun their opponents, and the 110–93 score sent shockwaves through the NBA. It was expected that Seattle wouldn't be so casual in Game 4, though.

As it happened, the Nuggets gave Seattle no option but to lose. The McNichols Sports Arena was electric that night, as the Denver crowd sensed what could possibly be the beginnings of a historical series. If the team won, the series would be tied at 2–2, with a one-off game left to decide the series.

Game 4 was tighter than the previous one. It went to overtime after a close battle, but to the amazement of everyone, the Nuggets took complete control soon after. In the end, they won it by nine points.

Everything was set up for a real squeaker back in Seattle.

Almost 15,000 SuperSonics fans turned up at the Seattle Center for the final game of the series, and they witnessed history. It wasn't the type of history they wanted to see, but it was memorable, nonetheless.

Another battle played out, with Seattle seemingly taking control in the fourth quarter. The Nuggets fought back as always, forcing Game 5 into overtime. Bison Dele, Robert Pack, and Reggie Williams were brilliant for the Nuggets, who managed to take control of the game in the final minutes. Denver held on to a 98–94 lead to complete one of the biggest upsets in NBA history.

Denver's underdog story didn't end there, though. In the semifinals, they dropped the first three games to the Utah Jazz, only to pull the series back to 3–3. Unfortunately, the gas tank finally ran dry, and they lost a close-fought Game 7.

The team's fairytale run was over, but they still had their history-making upset to keep them warm at night!

DID YOU KNOW...

The average height of an NBA player is 6 feet 6 inches (198.6cm), which is 8 inches taller than the average American man.

Air Jordans were actually banned in the NBA because they do not fit the color scheme. This did not stop Jordan from wearing them in 1984, causing him to get fined $5,000 each time.

James Naismith invented basketball in Springfield, Massachusetts in 1891.

The National Basketball League (NBL) and the Basketball Association of America (BAA) merged to form the NBA in 1949.

The first baskets used by James Naismith were peach baskets, which is where basketball got its name from. They did not even have holes in them to let the ball through.

Slam dunks were illegal from 1967 to 1976

Basketballs were generally brown until the late 1950s. They were changed to orange so that they were more visible.

The first Olympic basketball event was held in 1904, but it wasn't until 1936 that you could win an Olympic medal for basketball.

Two women have been drafted to play in the NBA. The first was Denise Long who was drafted in the 13th round by the San Francisco Warriors in 1969 and the second was Lusia Harris who was drafted in the 7th round in 1977 by the New Orleans Jazz.

Andrew Bynum became the youngest player ever to play in the NBA when he played in the 2005/06 season for the Lakers at the age of just 18 years and 6 days.

Basketball was originally played with a soccer ball.

The Golden State Warriors had the best-ever single regular season in 2015/16, recording 73 wins and 9 losses. Despite this unbelievable record, the Warriors lost the NBA Finals to the Cleveland Cavaliers, losing their last three games in the playoffs.

The NBA first adopted the 3-pointer in 1979 which it copied from the ABA.

LeBron James is the NBA's all-time top point scorer, after overtaking Kareem Abdul-Jabbar in career points in February 2023.

The Detroit Pistons and the Denver Nuggets played into three overtimes in 1983, setting the NBA points record with 370. The Pistons won 186-184.

The NBA logo silhouette is based on basketball legend Jerry West who played for the Los Angeles Lakers.

Wilt Chamberlain holds the record for the most points in a single game with an astonishing 100 points in 1962.

Michael Jordan is the wealthiest basketball player, with a net worth of $2 billion in 2023.

The highest recorded NBA attendance was on March 27, 1998, when 62,046 people went to watch the Chicago Bulls vs Atlanta Hawks.

Wilt Chamberlain holds the record for the most rebounds of all time with 23,924 over his career.

James Naismith released the official basketball rules in January 1892.

The first country to play basketball outside of America was Canada.

The University of Chicago and the University of Iowa were the first two universities to play a college game with five players in each team in 1896.

The longest NBA game happened in 1951 between Indianapolis Olympians and Rochester Royals, having six overtimes and taking 78 minutes.

The two tallest NBA players in history are Manute Bol and Gheorghe Muresan who stand at 7 foot 7 inches.

Muggsy Bogues is the shortest NBA player ever, standing at just 5 foot 3 inches.

Earl Lloyd was the first African-American to play in the NBA, doing so on October 31, 1950.

The first Chinese player to play in the NBA was Wang Zhizhi, doing so in the 2000-2001 season.

Ron Artest received one of the longest suspensions in NBA history for his aggressive behavior in a brawl when playing for the Indiana Pacers in 2004. He was suspended for 73 games as well as 13 playoff games, costing him $7 million in salary.

The WNBA was founded in 1996.

The Harlem Globetrotters were formed in 1926 and have been a huge part of basketball ever since. They have played over 26,000 games in 124 countries, but have never been a part of the NBA.

Basketball courts only officially had to be straight in 1903. Before that, they were often irregular shapes and sizes.

The IBF (International Basketball Federation) has a bounce requirement for a basketball. The ball must bounce between 3.9 ft and 4.6 ft when it is dropped from 5.9 ft.

The Los Angeles Lakers set the longest winning streak of NBA history in the 1971/72 season when they won 33 games in a row.

The Philadelphia 76ers hold the unfortunate record of having the longest losing streak in NBA history, losing 28 games in a row from 2014-15 to 2015-16.

The Memphis Grizzlies set the record for the largest winning margin in the 2021/22 season when they beat Oklahoma City Thunder by 73 points.

The most famous brawl in NBA history occurred in 2004 between the Pacers and the Pistons, involving a massive fight between the players and the spectators. As a result of this, nine players were suspended and five fans received criminal charges.

The shot clock was first introduced into the NBA in 1954.

Dribbling was introduced to basketball in 1901, however they were only allowed to bounce the ball once.

Steals and blocks only became an official NBA stat in 1973-74.

The first basketball game in Europe was in Paris in 1893.

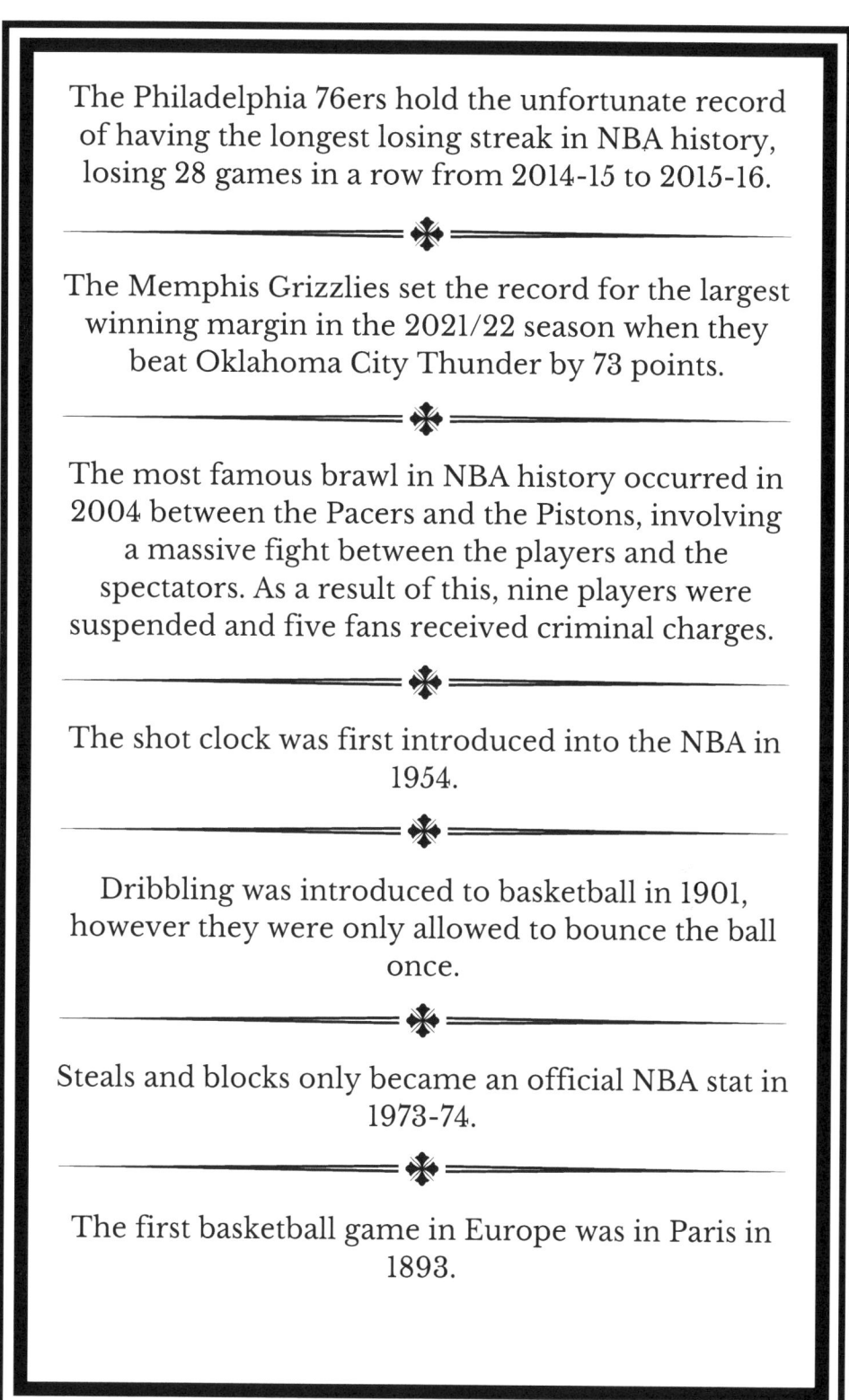

THE FINAL BUZZER

Sadly, that's the end of our journey through Basketball's Greatest Stories. Hopefully, you had some fun along the way, and maybe you learned something new in the process.

The NBA produces unbelievable stories all the time, and we love them all. But basketball is being played in thousands of courts in hundreds of countries all over the world, even as you read these words. Memories are being created constantly. Sports belong to everyone, and all standards are just as important as the next.

Who is to say that John Stockton's buzzer-beater in 1997 meant more to him than the feeling a kid gets making his first three-pointer? In truth, the joy each of them experiences is probably equal. It's what matters to the person making the shot that counts. Then there is the proud parent sitting in the bleachers as they watch their son or daughter make a game-winning point. To them, that shot is worth a million Kawhi Leonard buzzer-beaters!

And who could hear the story of J-Mac and not be inspired? The kid who struggled to step onto a court with nobody watching became an internet and international news sensation overnight when he played the game of his life in front of a camera and a packed high school arena! Nobody could have seen that coming, but that's what makes it so beautiful.

Jimmy Butler refused to hold a grudge, even though he was treated horribly at times during his childhood. His courage to let bygones be bygones can inspire all of us to forgive and forget when the time is right. He never let his troubles hold him back, and his life changed when he stumbled upon acceptance in a new friend's home. Jimmy found everything he'd been looking for in an overcrowded house full of love. His smile never faded, and he got his reward.

We've learned that Michael Jordan could win even when he was dehydrated and seriously ill! But it's probably a little unfair to compare ourselves to Mike, right? It sometimes feels unclear if Hollywood even used special effects for him in the original Space Jam movie! He was just that good.

Joking aside, we can take inspiration from anybody in life. The parent who works two jobs so their family can eat or the guy who stands in the rain holding a bucket for a charitable cause can also be the ones we look up to.

And you as well. You're an inspiration just for facing each day with a positive attitude. Life isn't always easy, and that's why we love to hear or read about the type of stories in this book. They help us to push forward, to dream, and to always believe.

And remember, often the falls we suffer make us strong in the end. Getting back up is the hardest thing to do in life, but it's the most rewarding part. Not one player mentioned in this book was handed the life and moments they created. They stumbled and fell many times, but they kept going. That's the only way to become what you deserve to be, and it's simply a part of life.

So, enjoy the good moments, and learn from the bad. And when things don't go your way, just shrug and think of CP3, Derek Fisher, or the Texas Western team that took on racism and won, and things will look brighter.

Always be inspired and be an inspiration yourself!

GLOSSARY

American Dream - The belief that anyone can be anything they want to be if they try hard enough. Equal opportunity.

Complacent - Careless, smug, or believing the bare minimum is acceptable.

Flamboyant - Confident and flashy.

Fundamentals - The basics and the essentials. Something can't work well without the fundamentals.

GOAT - The Greatest of All Time.

Hot Spot - A popular and busy place, usually a business or town.

Livid - Extremely angry.

Purple patch - A period of amazing success. A hot streak.

Respectively - In the same order as previously mentioned.

Segregation - Different races being kept separate, mostly in schools.

Shell-shocked - Stunned.

Stereotype - An image (usually an unfair one) created to paint a picture of a certain race or gender.

Work ethic - When someone always works hard, they have a good work ethic.

Printed in Great Britain
by Amazon